FU
Liberals

A journal for Conservatives
to destroy, rant and vent
without getting arrested

By Alex A. Lluch

WS Publishing Group
San Diego, California 92119

FU Liberals:
A journal for Conservatives to destroy,
rant and vent without getting arrested

By Alex A. Lluch
Published by WS Publishing Group
San Diego, California 92119
© Copyright 2010 by WS Publishing Group

Design by:
David Defenbaugh, Sarah Jang; WS Publishing Group

For more information on this and many other best-selling books visit
www.WSPublishingGroup.com.
E-mail: info@WSPublishingGroup.com

ISBN 13: 978-1-934386-98-9

Printed in China

 **W**rite a
WARNING
on this page to anyone who
finds this book.

O.B.A.M.A.

acro•nym
noun

1: formed from the initial letter
or letters of each of the parts
<I like to mock the president
with this acronym>

puzzle • wordgame • acrostic • composition

Complete this
ACRONYM:

O: ....

B: ....

A: ....

M: ....

A: ....

su•pe•ri•or
adjective

2: of higher rank, quality, or importance
4: excellent of its kind: better
<Republicans are clearly the superior party>

greater • excellent • high-caliber • first-rate • premium

List all the reasons Conservatives are SUPERIOR to Liberals.

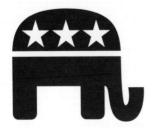

vs.

de•file
verb

1 a: to corrupt the purity or perfection of
<I will feel better after I defile this journal>

abuse • besmirch • dirty • pollute • sully • tarnish

Your face would look
much better like this

lue a picture of your most hated Democrat here and **<u>DEFILE</u>** it. Draw horns, fangs, or a mustache on it.

exile
verb

1: to be deported or forced
from one's country or home
<I would like to exile all
Liberals to Siberia>

banish • cast out • discard • oust • expulse • sayonara

Make a list of the annoying Liberal celebrities you wish would be EXILED to another country.

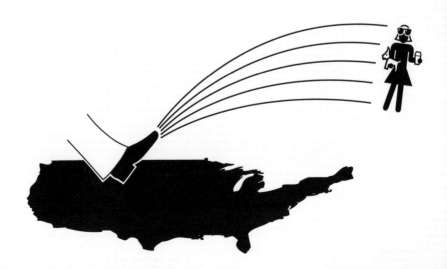

In•ter•net
noun

1: an electronic communications network
that connects computer networks around
the world
<Al Gore is so delusional he still thinks
he can take credit for the Internet>

Information Superhighway • World Wide Web

AL GORE

What is he best known for?

- ☐ Public speaking that puts people to sleep
- ☐ Losing his home state during the presidential election
- ☐ Spreading global warming propaganda
- ☐ Inventing the Internet

non•sen•si•cal
adjective

1 a: words or language having no meaning or
conveying no intelligible ideas
b: language, conduct, or an idea that is absurd
or contrary to good sense
<The speech he gave was totally nonsensical>

foolish • ridiculous • senseless • stupid • inane

Write down ✒
the most <u>NONSENSICAL</u> thing
you've heard a Liberal say recently.

"

"

im•mi•grants
noun

1: a person who becomes established in an
area where they were previously unknown
<Obama sympathizes with the immigrants>

outsider • foreigner • migrant • non-native

Check off the real reasons Obama wants to legalize illegal immigrants.

- ❏ He's kind and caring

- ❏ He wants to get more votes in the next election

- ❏ He wants to beef up the military

- ❏ He's forgotten how bad unemployment is

- ❏ He relates to being an illegal alien

- ❏ Write your own reason: ....
....
....

trick•ster
noun

1: a dishonest person who defrauds others
b: a cunning or deceptive character
<That trickster can't fool me with his
political jargon>

charlatan • con artist • imposter • cheat • swindler

You can't fool me, you TRICKSTER.

If you think the president has told some great lies, then call him out here.

chuck
verb

2 a: toss, throw
b: discard
c: dismiss, oust — used especially with 'out'
<I chucked this paper at my uncle's head>

toss • catapult • heave • throw • fling • lob

• • • Crumple this page into a ball and • • •

IT AT A LIBERAL YOU KNOW.

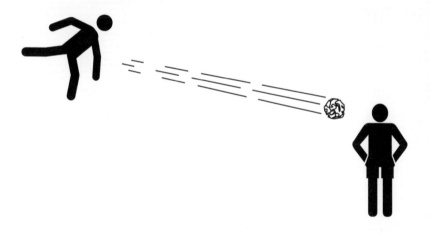

• • • Then walk away like it wasn't you. • • •

un•fair
adjective

1: marked by injustice
<It is completely unfair that
Obama is ruining our country>

awry • crooked • flawed • faulty • amiss • uncool

Write about the one **UNFAIR** law or bill that passed and how much that pisses you off.

res•cue
verb

1: to free from confinement, danger, or evil
<Someone please rescue me from Nancy>

salvage • liberate • free • relieve • get out

RESCUE ME!

What are three things you'd need if you were stranded on a desert island with Nancy Pelosi for eternity?

1 ....

2 ....

3 ....

swin•dle
verb

1: to take money or property from by fraud or deceit
<This country got swindled by the administration's
stimulus proposal>

cheat • con • trick • deceive • scam

THE ECONOMIC "SWINDLE US" PACKAGE INCLUDES:

- $20 billion for food stamp benefits

- $39 billion to subsidize health care insurance for the unemployed

- $6 billion for high-speed Internet to rural areas

- $6 billion to weatherize modest income homes

- $43 billion for extended unemployment benefits

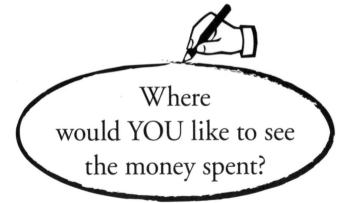

Where would YOU like to see the money spent?

hyp•o•crite
noun

2: a person who acts in contradiction
to his or her stated beliefs or feelings
<Everyone in politics is a hypocrite>

fraud • phony • two-faced • scammer • swindler

Show this HYPOCRITE
the bottom of your shoe.

(Stomp on this page !)

sar•cas•tic
adjective

1: joking or jesting often inappropriately
2: meant to be humorous or funny, not serious
<Can you tell my note was sarcastic?>

fake • false • guileful • insincere • phony • facetious

Write a **sarcastic** note

to everyone who doesn't vote.

Dear People
Who Don't Vote,

ter•ror•ist
noun

1: individuals or groups using terror as
a means of coercion
<Why don't we just bring the terrorists
to the U.S. and set them all free?>

radical • subversive • insurgent • rebel

Where would you like to send the Gitmo TERRORISTS after Obama closes the prison?

- ❑ White House lawn
- ❑ Air Force One hangar
- ❑ Al Gore's house
- ❑ Disneyland
- ❑ ACORN Headquarters
- ❑ To be Obama's Secret Service
- ❑ Hollywood

stream of con•scious•ness
noun

1: the continuous unedited
chronological flow of conscious
experience through the mind
<No one wants to be in my
stream of consciousness>

free association • inner monologue • train of thought

FU

STREAM OF CONSCIOUSNESS

Write the first thing that comes to your mind:

Health care reform: ....

....

Taxes: ....

....

War: ....

....

Gay marriage: ....

....

Global Warming: ....

....

Immigration: ....

....

Missile defense system: ....

....

Stem cell research: ....

....

Homeland Security: ....

....

des•pise
verb

1: to look down on with
contempt or aversion
<I despise Harry Reid>

abhor • disregard • scorn • loathe • dislike

Who is your most DESPISED political figure?

Label this voodoo doll as your most hated political figure. Tear it out, hang it on the wall, and throw darts at it.

in•com•mu•ni•ca•do
adverb

1: in a situation or state not allowing
communication
<The president was incommunicado; he must
have forgotten his Blackberry for 70 days>

missing in action • not speaking • silenced

70 DAYS
INCOMMUNICADO!

Make a list of all the really important reasons
Obama didn't have time to talk to
General McChrystal about Afghanistan.

- ❑ Training the White House dog

- ❑ Bringing the Olympics to Chicago

- ❑ Baking his daughter a birthday cake

- ❑ Working on his putting game

- ❑ Sitting courtside at a Lakers game

- ❑ Create your own reason: ....

....

....

suck
adjective

1: markedly inferior in quality :
lousy, inadequate
<Could this administration
suck any more?>

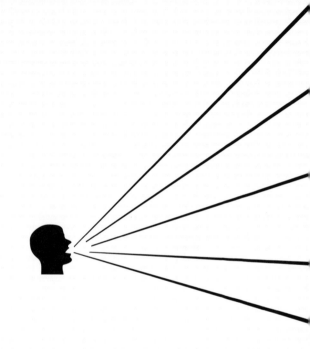

crummy • junky • lousy • shoddy • inferior • third rate

YOU
SUCK
!!!!!!!!!!!
● ● ● ● ● ● ● ● ● ● ●

Yell "You suck!" as loud as
you can into these pages.

(Don't do this at a political rally
or you may get arrested.)

out•source
verb

1: to procure under contract with
an outside supplier
<It seems pretty stupid to outsource
so many jobs when unemployment
is at 10 percent>

send out • reassign • distribute • dispatch

SECRETARY
OF STATE

Hillary
Clinton

What is she best known for?

☐ Wearing really nice pantsuits

☐ Being married to former President Bill Clinton

☐ The Monica Lewinsky and Whitewater scandals

☐ Apologizing to India for the "U.S.'s mistakes,"
when we continue to outsource our jobs there

swap
verb

1 a: to give in trade
<I want to swap the president
for George Clooney>

barter • exchange • switch • trade • flip

If you could
SWAP

this president and vice president
for celebrities, who would
you choose?

....

(celebrity president)

....

(celebrity vice president)

cel•e•brate
verb

2 a: to honor by refraining from ordinary business
b: to mark by festivities or other deviation from routine
<I plan to celebrate the fact that you were impeached>

party • paint the town red • let loose • rejoice • fiesta

 CELEBRATE!

Pretend the Democrat who sucks
the most is getting impeached.

 Tear this page into tiny pieces of confetti
and throw them up in the air to celebrate.

global warm•ing
noun

1: an alleged increase in the
earth's atmospheric and oceanic
temperatures due to pollution
<Global warming is just another
Liberal scare tactic>

hype • propaganda • hogwash • rubbish

GLOBAL WARMING IS:

☐ A sad reality

☐ Earth's natural cycle

☐ A huge lie

☐ A way to put fear in people

☐ Al Gore's meal ticket

be•rate
verb

1: to scold or condemn
vehemently and at length
<I will berate you with
this letter>

badmouth • bash • slam • offend • smear • zing

Berate a Liberal of your choice.

Dear ....,

You suck so much, I want to throw
.... at you.
Listening to you speak makes me want
to ....
When I found out you got elected,
I wanted to ....
A .... would be better
in office than you. Why don't you
move to ....
for .... years?

Sincerely,

....

qual•i•fied
adjective

1: training or experience for a given purpose
<How about we find someone who is
actually qualified to oversee the IRS>

expert • capable • experienced • appropriate

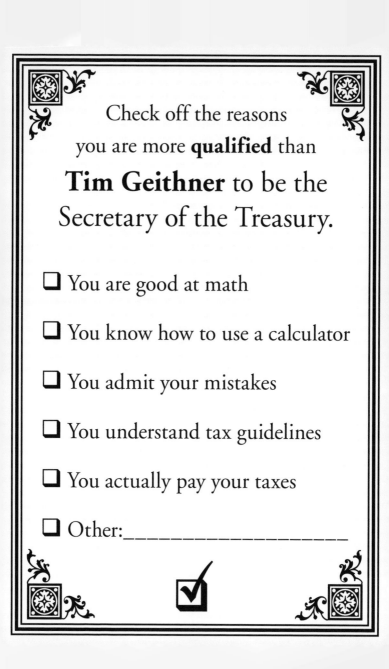

Check off the reasons
you are more **qualified** than
Tim Geithner to be the
Secretary of the Treasury.

❏ You are good at math

❏ You know how to use a calculator

❏ You admit your mistakes

❏ You understand tax guidelines

❏ You actually pay your taxes

❏ Other:_____

brain•storm•ing
verb

1: the mulling over of ideas
<I enjoy brainstorming ways to smack
down the Obama administration>

analyze • conceive • put heads together • concoct

FU Brainstorming Session

whiny

elitist intellectuals

losers

Vandalize this page with all the
words that describe Liberals.

double agent
noun

1: a spy pretending to serve one political
party while actually serving another
<I suspect Joe Lieberman is a double agent>

inside man • spy • mole • undercover agent • informer

DOUBLE AGENT

What Democrat do you suspect
is secretly on your side?

_____

_____

_____

_____

_____

_____

crash•ers
noun

1: a person who enters, attends, or participates
without ticket or invitation
<Joe Biden is so oblivious he was hugging
the White House party crashers>

infiltrator • intruder • snooper • trespasser

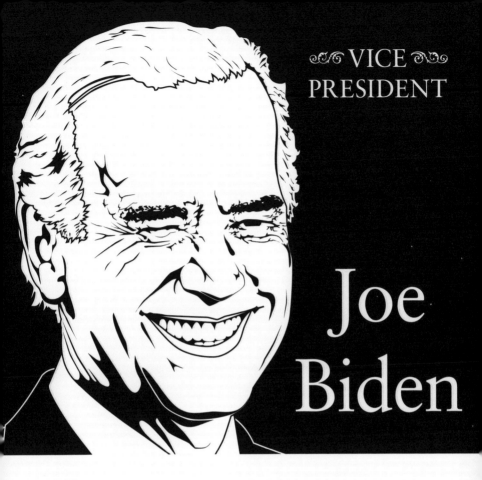

Joe Biden

What is he best known for?

- ☐ Telling Americans not to fly or take the subway for fear of swine flu. Whoops.

- ☐ Accidentally revealing the location of the vice presidential top-secret bunker

- ☐ Having hair plugs

- ☐ Taking photos with his arms around the White House State Dinner party crashers

ex•tinct
adjective

2: no longer existing
<I hope the Liberals won't miss their avocados
when the California farmers become extinct>

obsolete • gone • defunct • missing • snuffed out

Decide who gets the water and who goes EXTINCT.

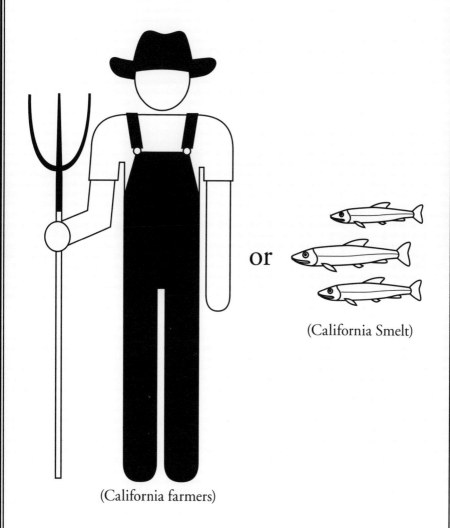

or

(California Smelt)

(California farmers)

Draw an X to indicate who bites the dust.

award
noun

2: something that is conferred or
bestowed especially on the basis of merit
<I present you with the award for
the shadiest Liberal ever>

distinction • honor • prize • badge • accolade • ribbon

Give someone this AWARD.

CONGRATULATIONS

_____!

You have won the distinction of dumbest Liberal on the planet.

#1 Loser

spell
noun

1 a: spoken word or set of words
believed to have magic power
<I cast a spell on him; he will
now turn into a pig>

hex • conjuring • magic • mojo • sorcery • wizardry • jinx

CAST A SPELL

on a Liberal who annoys
the crap out of you.

INSTRUCTIONS:

- Pour ½ cup of red wine into a bowl.
- Break a pen and pour the ink into the mixture.
- Add two dashes of garlic salt.
- Drop in a pinch of staples.
- Mix counterclockwise.

Now, check off which effect you want the spell to have on your foe.

☐ A week of bad luck

☐ Can't find his or her car keys

☐ Grow a tail

☐ Smell like rotten fish

back off
verb

1: to withdraw from a position
<I told my coworker to back off
with the political rants>

retreat • resign • yield • wither • submit • fend off

Back Off!

Tell Liberals how you feel. Trace your hand on this page with
your middle finger raised and decorate it.

fan•tasy
noun

1: the power or process of creating
especially unrealistic or improbable
mental images
<In my fantasy, there are no
Liberals in government>

daydream • utopia • fairytale • dream • bubble

Fill out your **fantasy** ballot.

President: ....

Vice President: ....

Secretary of State: ....

Secretary of the Treasury: ....

Attorney General: ....

Secretary of Defense: ....

Secretary of Homeland Security: ....

Governor of your state: ....

.................................: ....

.................................: ....

.................................: ....

cer•tif•i•cate
noun

1: a document containing a certified
statement as to the truth of something
<Why won't he present a birth certificate?>

document • proof • testimonial • guarantee

𝕭𝖎𝖗𝖙𝖍 𝕮𝖊𝖗𝖙𝖎𝖋𝖎𝖈𝖆𝖙𝖊

This certifies that

Barack Hussein Obama

Was born:

- ❏ Honolulu, Hawaii
- ❏ The Middle East somewhere
- ❏ Antarctica
- ❏ Timbuktu, Africa
- ❏ Definitely not in the U.S.
- ❏ On another planet, probably Mars
- ❏ Other:_____

★ OFFICIAL ★

civil rights
noun

1: the rights of personal liberty guaranteed to
United States citizens by the Constitution
<Barney Frank pretends to care about our
civil rights but really only cares about pot>

liberties • freedoms • fairness • equality

CONGRESSMAN
Barney Frank

What is he best known for?

- ☐ Being an openly gay senator
- ☐ Defending civil rights
- ☐ Campaigning for legalizing marijuana
- ☐ Dating a male prostitute and paying off his parking tickets

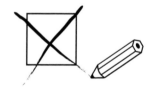

buzz•word
noun

1: an important-sounding usually technical word or phrase often of little meaning used chiefly to impress laymen
<I can't make sense of Liberal buzzwords>

bunk • cliché • mumbo jumbo • lingo • nonsense

BUZZWORD

Social Justice	Public Option	Tolerant	Progressive	Civilian Army
Hope	Transparency	Czar	Fairness Doctrine	Equality
Think Outside the Box	Reform	**FREE SPACE**	Fearmonger	Going Green
Welfare	Pro-Choice	Visionary	Immigration Reform	Change
Global Warming	Agenda	Diversity	Synergy	Grassroots

BiNGO
FU

Put an X through the box each time you hear annoying Liberal jargon.

loos•en up
verb

1: to become less tense
<I need to loosen up with a stiff drink>

balm • pacify • placate • calm • tranquilize • ease

Loosen the
F#@K UP

Make a list of the ways you can
get your mind off politics.

syn•o•nym
noun

1: one of two or more words or expressions of
the same language that have the same meaning
<Match these synonyms, if you can wade
through the Liberal propaganda>

equivalent • correlation • match • parallel • sameness

FU Synonyms

Match the words with their real definitions.

Illegal aliens	Grassroots
Astroturf	Nickels & dimes
Progressive	Common sense
Change	Nonqualified employees
Czar	Future Liberal voters
Green Movement	Marxist
Global Warming	Opening the border
Foreign Relations	Hoax
Immigration Reform	Another form of taxes
Republicans	Apologizing to our enemies

pissed
adjective

1: bitter in spirit: irritated
<Caution: Pissed off
Conservative behind the wheel>

bitter • dismal • crestfallen • annoyed • dejected

Pissed off?

Warn Liberals to stay back from your car. Create bumper stickers about your most hated politicians.

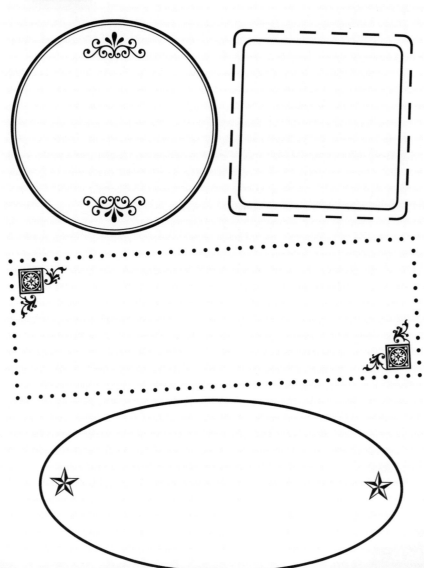

acorn
noun

1: the nut of the oak
<ACORN is nuts alright>

nut • crazy • corrupt • illegal • fraudulent

ACORN

— TRUE OR FALSE —

T or **F**

❑ ❑ Tax loopholes for prostitutes

❑ ❑ Committed voter fraud

❑ ❑ Helped Obama win the election

❑ ❑ Gave homeless people cigarettes and alcohol for votes

❑ ❑ Corrupt organization

❑ ❑ A waste of taxpayer money

haz•ard
noun

1: a source of danger
<Liberals are a hazard to my health>

imperilment • jeopardy • peril • risk • thin ice

EXTREME
HEALTH <u>HAZARD</u>

Do **NOT** Reelect

....

He/She is

....

....

and poses extreme danger to

....

....

....

crush
noun

3 a: an intense and usually
passing infatuation
b: the object of infatuation
<None of my Republican friends
can know of my crush>

flame • love affair • passion • puppy love • enamor

Is there a Liberal political figure or activist you have a secret

CRUSH

on?

We'll never tell …

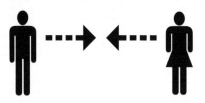

pin
verb

2: to assign the blame
or responsibility for
<I'd like to pin the
blame on the Liberals>

stick • attach • fasten • affix • press

Pin the Tie on the Donkey

Tear out this sheet. Hang it on the wall.

po•lit•i•cal
adjective

1: the conduct of someone with
questionable and tactical motives
<Hillary's decisions are purely political>

cunning • crafty • tactical • calculated • strategic

Political Word Search

t	r	b	i	r	i	l	t	i	b	f	v	a
n	d	b	e	t	a	b	e	d	v	a	d	t
e	v	i	t	a	v	r	e	s	n	o	c	u
m	i	l	y	n	o	f	c	l	n	n	c	n
n	h	l	i	b	e	r	a	l	y	d	l	n
o	l	c	s	n	m	d	m	c	c	a	i	n
r	s	e	s	s	n	r	i	c	n	b	n	y
i	p	e	a	a	e	l	s	s	t	v	t	m
v	u	h	c	r	o	r	p	e	e	i	o	o
n	n	s	k	p	s	s	g	t	n	r	n	n
e	d	u	c	a	t	i	o	n	s	a	p	o
a	i	b	e	y	a	m	a	b	o	q	t	c
e	t	a	b	e	d	h	n	n	i	c	a	e

Liberal	Senate	Debate	Iraq
Conservative	Congress	Environment	Israel
Policy	Pundit	Clinton	Hannity
Bill	Defense	Obama	Beck
President	Economy	McCain	Scandal
Veto	Education	Bush	Debate

scrib•ble
verb

1: to write hastily or carelessly without regard
to legibility or form
2: to cover with careless or worthless writings
or drawings
<When I scribble in this journal, I feel better>

doodle • jot • scratch • scrawl • squiggle

Scribble

on this page as hard
as you can.

Take out your frustration with this
administration here.

blunt
adjective

3 a: abrupt in speech or manner
b: being straight to the point
<Let me be blunt: You all suck>

direct • unsubtle • outspoken • honest • candid

Draft the email you wish you could send to all your irrational Liberal friends.

Subject: The **Blunt** Truth

To: All my Liberal friends

Cc: Democratic Party

Send

big cheese
noun

1: boss; in charge
<FU Liberals; I am
the big cheese now>

boss • chief • head honcho • leader • president • VIP

BIG CHEESE

Bye bye, Obama. Pretend YOU are the new president of the United States. How would you solve the health care reform crisis?

cir•cum•vent
verb

2: to manage to get around especially
by ingenuity or stratagem
<This maze reminds me of how the
president circumvents tough questions>

skirt • evade • sidestep • bypass • dodge • avoid

Make your way through this maze
to the White House, but be sure to
➤ CIRCUMVENT ➤
all the Liberal crap.

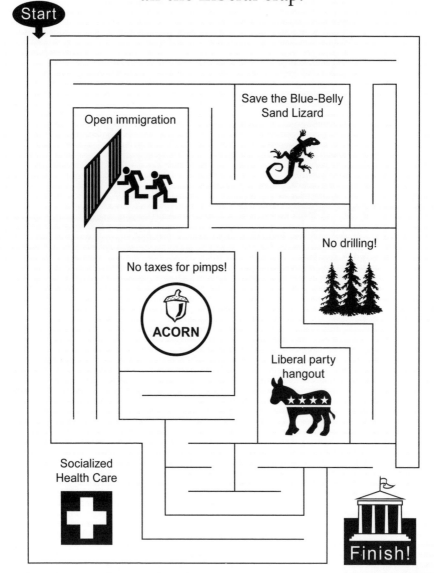

czar
noun

1: one having great
power or authority
<Obama should make
me the Czar of Czars>

authority • expert • governor • big wig

CROSS OUT THE 4 FAKE
CZARS

Yes, the rest are Obama's actual Czars! More than any president in history.

Afghanistan Czar	Guantanamo Closure Czar
AIDS Czar	Health Czar
Auto Recovery Czar	Information Czar
Bowling Czar	Intelligence Czar
Border Czar	Mideast Peace Czar
California Water Czar	Pay Czar
Car Czar	Pilates Czar
Czar of Czars	Regulatory Czar
Central Region Czar	Science Czar
Climate Czar	Stimulus Accountability Czar
Domestic Violence Czar	Sudan Czar
Drug Czar	TARP Czar
Economic Czar	Technology Czar
Energy and Environment Czar	Terrorism Czar
Faith-Based Czar	Urban Affairs Czar
Government Performance Czar	Weapons Czar
Great Lakes Czar	WMD Policy Czar
Green Jobs Czar	Video Game Czar

Fake Czars: Bowling Czar, Czar of Czars, Pilates Czar, Video Game Czar

na•tion•al se•cu•ri•ty
noun

1: the quality or state of the country
being secure
2: freedom from danger for terrorism
<Eric Holder doesn't give a crap
about national security, does he>

protection • safekeeping • sanctuary • preservation

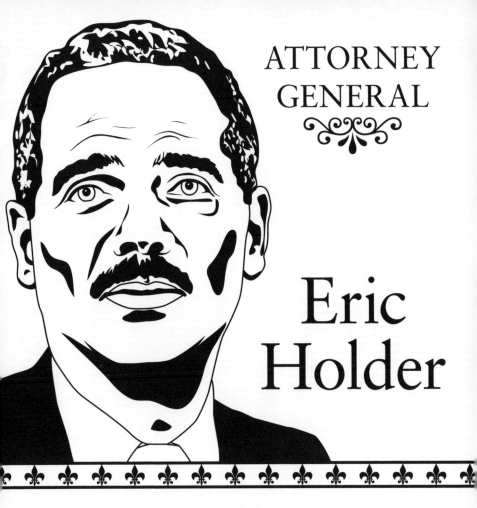

ATTORNEY GENERAL

Eric Holder

What is he best known for?

- ❑ The first African-American to be Attorney General

- ❑ Pardoning billionaire fugitive Marc Rich

- ❑ Seizing 6-year-old Elian Gonzalez at gunpoint and sending him back to Cuba

- ❑ Releasing private memos from the Bush administration on torture, damaging national security

picket
verb

1: to protest against for a cause
<I would like to picket against
saving the tree frogs>

boycott • demonstrate • strike • hit the bricks • protest

FU PICKET SIGN

Create a
picket sign
to protest the
most annoying
Liberal issue.

cheap shot
noun

2: a critical statement that takes unfair advantage of a known weakness of the target <I'd like to take a cheap shot at Nancy Pelosi>

backbite • knock • hit • slander • snub

FU
Cheap Shot

Pretend you are running a smear campaign against
your most hated Liberal politician.
Make a list of the politician's faults and screw ups.

....

....

....

....

....

....

....

....

....

....

....

....

....

....

blood•bath
noun

2: a notably fierce, violent, or
destructive contest or struggle
<A fight between Ann Coulter
and President Obama would
be a bloodbath>

massacre • carnage • slaughter • annihilation • fight

Let the **Bloodbath** Begin!

Write who you would like to see go head-to-head in a boxing match.

In the Liberal corner we have …

In the Conservative corner we have …

al•lo•cate
verb

1: to apportion for a specific purpose
or to particular persons or things
<I would allocate half the budget for
ice cream research>

allot • assign • divvy • dish out • slice • share

FU Budget Allocation

Forget saving the manatees; write down how you would like the government to spend YOUR tax money.

Don't spend it all in one place!

Cut out this slip and mail it with your taxes in April.

qual•i•fi•ca•tions
noun

1: a condition or standard that
must be complied with
<Apparently you don't need
qualifications to be one of the
president's advisors>

ability • skill • quality • competence • goods

Match these people's QUALIFICATIONS to their jobs.

Lawyer	15 years of medical school and medical residencies, head of surgery at Johns Hopkins
Advertising Executive	Host of a campus radio show, dropped out of Yale a few credits short of graduation, once slept in his car in a GM parking lot
Neurosurgeon	MBA from Columbia, creator of award-winning campaigns
Special Assistant to the President, Restructuring GM and the American Auto Industry	JD from Yale, partner in major law firm, published author

mot•to

noun

1: a sentence, phrase, or word inscribed on
something as appropriate to or indicative of its
character or use
<My campaign motto would be "FU Liberals">

slogan • aphorism • byword • epigram • maxim • proverb

CAMPAIGN MOTTO

If you were running for president,
what would your slogan be?

los•er
noun

1: a person or thing that loses especially consistently
2: a person who is incompetent or unable to
succeed; something doomed to fail or disappoint
<These Bleeding Heart Liberals are losers>

dud • failure • deadbeat • flop • flunkee • waste of space

Biggest Liberal Loser

Liberal most likely to …

Embezzle money: ....

Have a secret love child: ....

Bungle a foreign leader's name: ....

Fall down the stairs at a speech: ....

Come out of the closet: ....

Waste our tax money: ....

Be forced out of office: ....

doomed
adjective

2: to make certain the failure or destruction of
<This administration will be doomed by the
terrible way they handled the bailout>

condemned • hopeless • sunk • dead duck

Chris Dodd

What is he best known for?

- ❑ Owning a cozy cottage in the Irish countryside

- ❑ Being the son of a senator who was dismissed for using campaign funds for personal use

- ❑ Receiving shady "VIP loans" from doomed lender Countrywide Financial

- ❑ Allowing AIG executives to receive bonuses using federal bailout money

guilty
adjective

1: responsible for a grave
breach of conduct
<This administration is
guilty of a lot of shadiness>

blameworthy • liable • at fault • shady

GUILTY BY ASSOCIATION

List all the corrupt people
Obama associates with:

rather
adverb

1: more readily or willingly
<I would rather eat dog food
than become a Democrat>

considerably • noticeably • quite • much

Would you **rather** ...

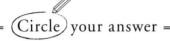

Become a Democrat	- or -	Eat dog food
Go on a date with Ann Coulter	- or -	Date Hillary Clinton
Open the border to immigrants	- or -	Move to Fallujah
Have drinks with Bill Clinton	- or -	Go hunting with Dick Cheney
Lobby for saving tree frogs	- or -	Swim with sharks
Have a televised debate with Bill O'Reilly	- or -	Debate Bill Maher
Be appointed to the Supreme Court	- or -	Be Vice President
Legalize marijuana	- or -	Nationalize health care

cre•a•tive
adjective

1: the ability to be artistic;
imaginative
<This journal lets me be
creative while venting>

clever • inspired • productive • imaginative • visionary

FU Creative Writing Assignment

Complete this poem.
There once was a Liberal
from Nantucket ...

....
....
....
....
....
....
....
....

lib•eral

noun

1: not strict in the observance of orthodox, traditional, or established forms or ways <"Liberal" is a dirty word>

permissive • passive • socialist • pushover

Liberal Stimulus Package Part II

Check off the possible Liberal ideas for increasing government revenue.

○ Legalize marijuana

○ Legalize cocaine

○ Legalize prostitution

○ Lower drinking age to 16

○ Destroy thousands of "clunkers"

○ Legalize gambling nationwide

○ Sell Obama bobblehead dolls

bar•ring
verb

1: limiting, preventing from
<Harry Reid is really barring this nation
from making any progress. Ass.>

prevent • prohibit • frustrate • hinder • block

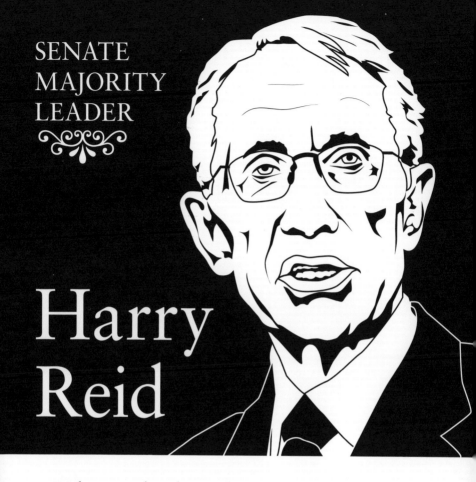

SENATE
MAJORITY
LEADER

Harry Reid

What is he best known for?

❑ Being a Mormon Liberal

❑ Viciously opposing the Iraqi war

❑ Barring Senators from borrowing corporate jets for travel

❑ Using campaign donations to buy Christmas presents for his condo's employees

Ha
ha
ha

joke
noun

1: a brief oral narrative with a climactic
humorous twist
b: the humorous or ridiculous element in
something
<I like making a joke at a Liberal's expense>

prank • farce • humor • shenanigan • wisecrack

Tell your favorite
Liberal-bashing joke.

Ha
ha
ha

Q: What is the difference between a Liberal and a pig?

A: One is fat, smelly, and squeals loudly, and the other is a farm animal.

Q: ....

....

....

A: ....

....

....

cra•zy
adjective

2: mad, insane
<Rev. Wright is obviously
completely crazy>

batty • insane • nuts • losing it • ranting

W.W.R.W.D.

(What Would Reverend Wright Do?)

What's the CRAZIEST thing you heard Obama's mentor of 20 years say during the election?

"America's chickens are coming home to roost."

"Racism is how this country was founded and how this country is still run!… We [in the U.S.] believe in white supremacy and black inferiority and believe it more than we believe in God."

~ Reverend Wright

"Bill Clinton did us, just like he did Monica Lewinsky. He was riding dirty."

pro•pa•gan•da
noun

1: the spreading of ideas, information, or rumor for the purpose of injuring an institution, a cause, or a person
2: ideas, facts, or allegations spread deliberately to further one's cause or to damage an opposing cause
<Liberals want to brainwash us with propaganda>

hype • disinformation • hogwash • publicity

Cover this page with all the annoying Liberal **propaganda** you can find ...

No Guns Allowed!

Forget about your constitutional right!

No Citizenship? No Problem!

Relief for all!

No Drilling!

Alternative fuel only!

im•pale
verb

2: to pierce with
something pointed
<I will impale this
voodoo doll with pins>

lance • prick • skewer • spike • stick • gouge

prize
noun

1: an award or winnings given
for an accomplishment
<What exactly did the president
do to deserve this prize?>

award • champ • elite • laurel • privilege

If Obama can win a **Nobel Peace Prize** for doing NOTHING, so can you!

ALFR. NOBEL

I hereby award myself the
Nobel Peace Prize for

_____

_____

_____

_____

_____

bi•as
adjective

1: a personal and sometimes unreasoned
judgment or slant
2: an instance of prejudice
<It is so obvious that he is a bias Liberal>

favoritism • slant • unfairness • one-sided • blinded

MICHAEL MOORE

What is he best known for?

❑ Being fat, pushy and Anti-American.

❑ Handing out underwear and ramen noodles to young people in Michigan to get them to vote.

❑ Creator of dishonest and disingenuous films, such as Fahrenheit 911 and Bowling for Columbine.

❑ Claiming the Bush family has close personal ties to Osama Bin Laden.

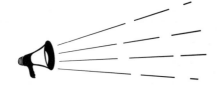

shut up
verb

1: to cause a person to
stop talking
<I wish I could tell my
Liberal friend to shut up>

clam up • hush • quiet down • zip it • settle • refrain

shut UP!

 Point this page at your Liberal friends the next time they are complaining to you.

mis•rep•re•sen•ta•tion
noun

1: to give a false or misleading representation of,
usually with an intent to deceive or be unfair
<Michael Moore's crappy movies are a
misrepresentation of Conservatives>

falsehood • distortion • false light • slant • lie

FU Liberal Misrepresentation

Dispel one of the most popular Liberal
misconceptions about Conservatives.

skip
verb

1: to pass over or omit a necessary interval,
item, or step
<Don't worry if you skip out on your taxes,
you can still be Secretary of the Treasury>

avoid • disregard • play hooky • skim over

Tim Geithner

What is he best known for?

- ☐ Distributing billions of dollars to failing banks and insurance companies

- ☐ Having great hair

- ☐ Hiring an illegal alien to work for him

- ☐ Skipping out on his self-employment taxes

blind
adjective

1: unable or unwilling to discern or judge
2: having no regard to rational discrimination,
guidance, or restriction
<I refuse to turn a blind eye to how sucky
this administration is>

unquestioning • thoughtless • in the dark

SIGN BLIND

Pretend you're a Congressman. Get a pen.
Blindfold yourself. Now sign this health care
bill without reading it.

Proposed
Health Care Bill

....

SIGNATURE

Now you just acted as our
trusted Congressmen.

ex•cit•ing
adjective

1: causing great enthusiasm
and eagerness
<I enjoy an exciting
election, unless we lose>

thrilling • exhilarating • rousing • stimulating • gripping

 all the words that
describe the last election.

Bogus   Intense   CRIMINAL

Stupid

Unfair   Competitive   AWESOME

EXCITING

CUTTHROAT   Pointless

Victorious   SENSIBLE

Despicable

Neck in Neck   Ruthless

Outrageous

SLANDEROUS

Scary   Hopeful   Rotten

pow•er hun•gry
adjective

1: having an insatiable desire for
wealth and power
<Nancy Pelosi is so power-hungry
she will stop at nothing to get
what she wants>

greedy • carnivorous • acquisitive • devouring

SPEAKER OF THE HOUSE

Nancy Pelosi

What is she best known for?

❏ Eating a pint of chocolate ice cream daily

❏ Being the first female Speaker of the House, and also second in line for the presidency (Shudder)

❏ Defeating the privatization of Social Security

❏ Being a power-hungry Liberal who is one of the richest politicians in the House

im•pres•sion
noun

1: an imitation or
representation of someone
<My impression isn't as
crazy as the real Obama>

imitation • parody • representation • pretending

Cut out this mask and do your very best Barack Obama **IMPRESSION.** Entertain all your Conservative friends.

mas•cot
noun

1: a person, animal, or thing adopted
by a group as a symbolic figure
<The donkey is a perfect mascot,
because Democrats are asses>

representation • symbol • charm • object